Family Stories to Tell

by Terry Miller Shannon

All families have stories to tell. They have stories from the past.

3

We can learn about
our family's stories in many ways.
We can look at old pictures.

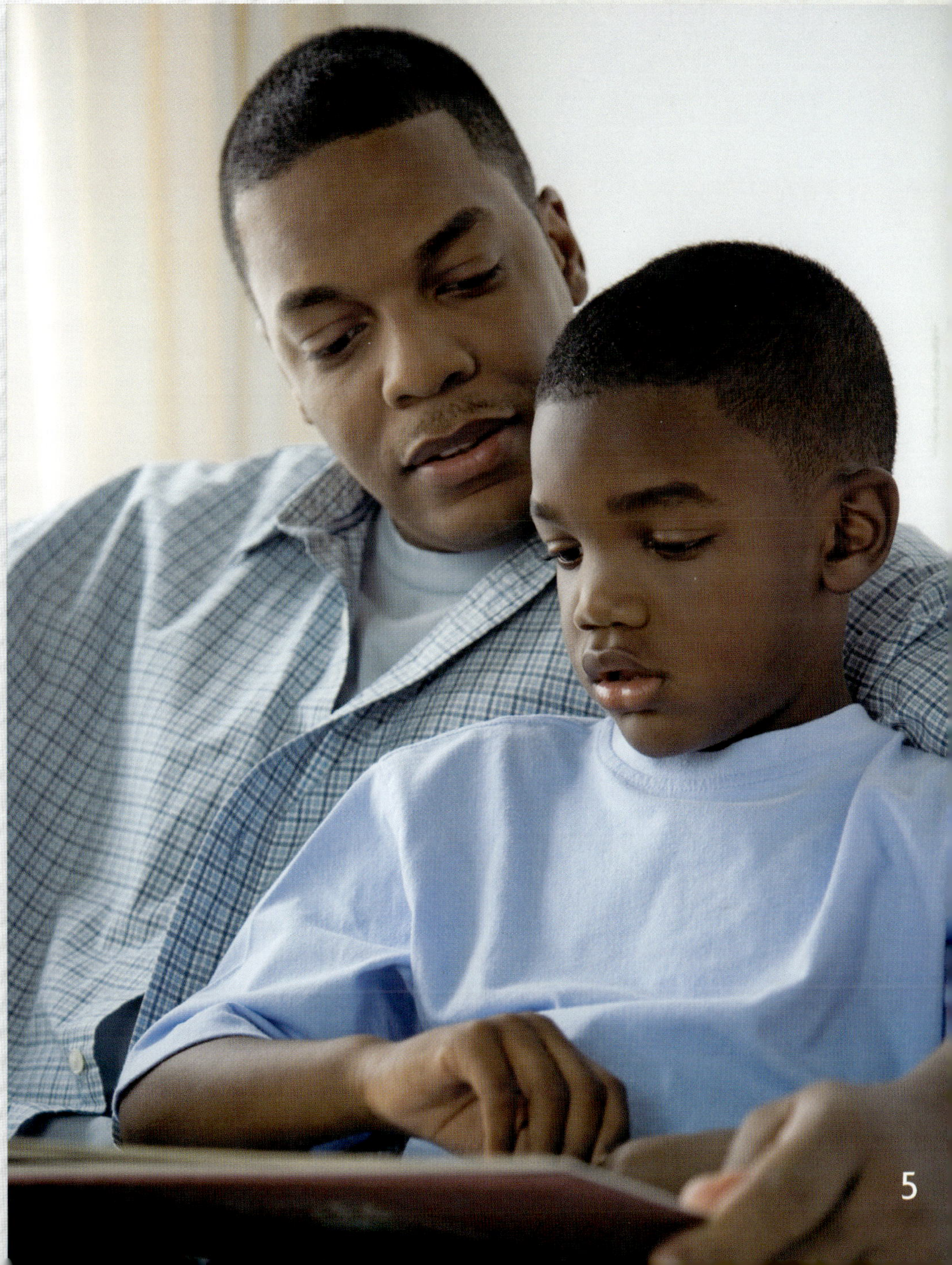

We can ask our grandparents questions.

We can find out where they grew up.

7

Some families have
old newspapers.
We can read them to learn
about the past.
We might read about our family.

STUDY FINDS NEW TREATMENT FOR DISEASE

Scientist Wins Award for Research

NEWS-REGISTER

Ceremony Wednesday

ase join in ating the nts of Dr. Town rmony PM.

Some families have old school report cards.
We can ask questions about what school was like.

11

Some families have old home movies. We can learn about our family by watching home movies.

13

We can play old records.
Our family can tell us
about the music they liked.

15

Families have many stories to tell. They can tell them in many ways.